STO

(31) Firebox
(32) Back driving wheels
(33) Wheel spokes
(34) Driving wheel guard
(35) Safety chains
(36) Cab foot steps

(37) Water suction p[...]
(38) Draw bar
(39) Cab handholds
(40) Cab
(41) Cab front door
(42) Injector steam pipe

(45) Water gauge
(46) Reversing lever
(47) Steam gauge
(48) Gauge cocks

(49) Furnace door
(50) Sandbox valve handle
(51) Whistle lever
(52) Footboard
(53) Cab support
(54) Safety valve

(55) Whistle
(56) Dome
(57) Injector feed pipe
(58) Injector check valve
(59) Boiler
(60) Cladding plate band
(61) Runningboard
(62) Handrail
(63) Handrail column
(64) Sandbox
(65) Sand pipes
(66) Bell
(67) Bell cord
(68) Smokestack
(69) Smokebox
(70) Cleanout

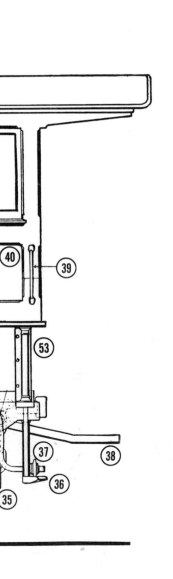

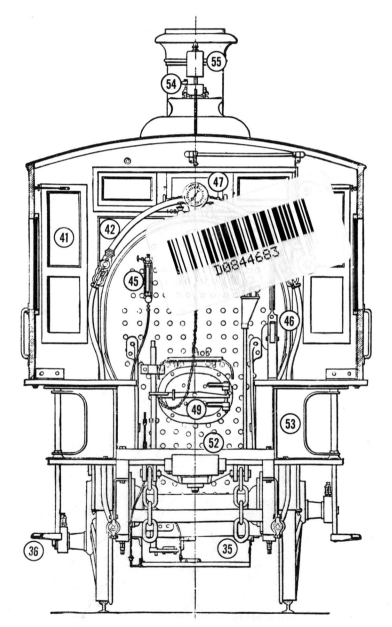

LOCOMOTIVE
~ BUILDING AN EIGHT-WHEELER ~

RICH.ᴰ NORRIS & SON
LOCOMOTIVE WORKS

BOILER SHOP

LOCOMOTIVE

~ BUILDING AN EIGHT-WHEELER ~

DAVID WEITZMAN

HOUGHTON MIFFLIN COMPANY
BOSTON 1999

BALTIMORE, MARYLAND. AUGUST 28, 1830. Today is the trial run of Peter Cooper's locomotive, Tom Thumb. It's to be a race between a steam locomotive and a horse, and the winner will be chosen by the Baltimore & Ohio Railroad to pull its freight and passenger trains.

Peter is the engineer. He starts a fire under the little boiler with kindling and cordwood, and pumps water from a barrel into the boiler. Behind Tom Thumb is an open, boat-shaped car filled with the railroad's directors. The steam hisses from the boiler, the horse prances impatiently, the pressure and excitement mount until suddenly Tom Thumb and its startled passengers lurch off down the track.

Tom Thumb overtakes the horse and speeds toward the finish line, but suddenly a drive belt snaps and the engine rolls to a wheezing stop. Although Peter Cooper lost the race, he would win in the long run: the steam locomotive, not the horse, would power American railroads in years to come.

Still, not even Peter could imagine how steam engines and railroads would grow. Our first locomotives came from England, built by Robert Stephenson & Company. But soon Americans were making their own. Anyone, it seemed, could build one. Locomotives were built in smithies, foundries, carriage shops, and even stables, some of the first by a grocery clerk, a dry-goods merchant, a mathematics teacher, a jeweler, a watch-maker, and a tinker.

By 1840, there were more miles of railroad track in the United States than in all the countries of Europe combined. By the mid-1850s, the tracks reached the Midwest, and passenger trains brought immigrants from all over the world to Chicago, Kansas City, and St. Louis. By the 1870s, Americans were building the biggest, most powerful locomotives in the world—and more of them.

This is where our story begins.

The year is 1870, just a few months after laborers complete the transcontinental railroad. When two locomotives touch cowcatchers at Promontory Point, Utah, America is joined east to west by rail, and a web of new lines spreads all over the nation. New routes require more equipment, and factories are turning out a locomotive every two days. One of the most useful locomotives of the day is a wood-burning 4-4-0.

First, a new locomotive is built with lines on paper. Each is custom designed. Will the locomotive be used for freight or passenger service or perhaps both? Will it burn wood or coal? Will the locomotive travel

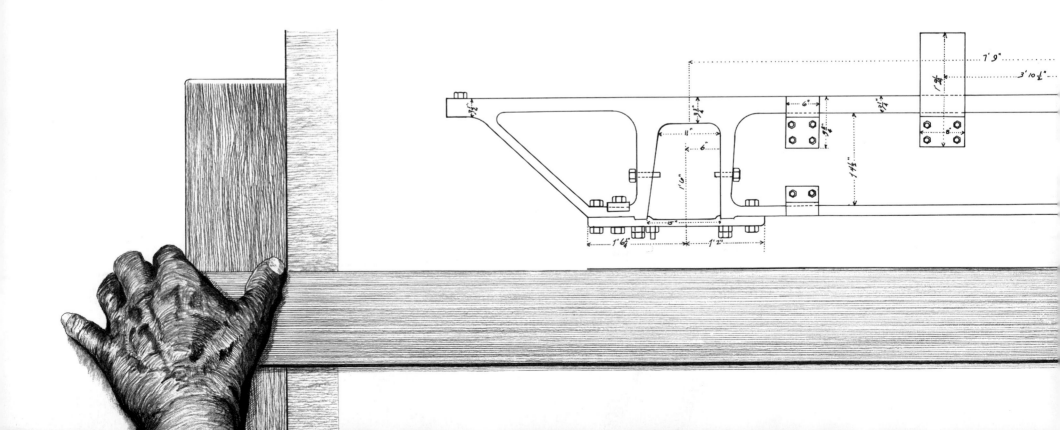

a flat and straight route or will it have to go around tight curves and climb steep mountain grades? How many wheels will it have? The master mechanic uses this information to draft the design.

The master mechanic begins with a large elevation drawing. From this, draftsmen make smaller drawings of the more than six thousand locomotive parts for the craftsmen who will be making them. For simple parts, quick sketches suffice.

Each drawing is glued to heavy cardboard and stored in the drawing room. When a worker begins a part, he checks out the drawing and mounts it on the wall near his machine tool or workbench.

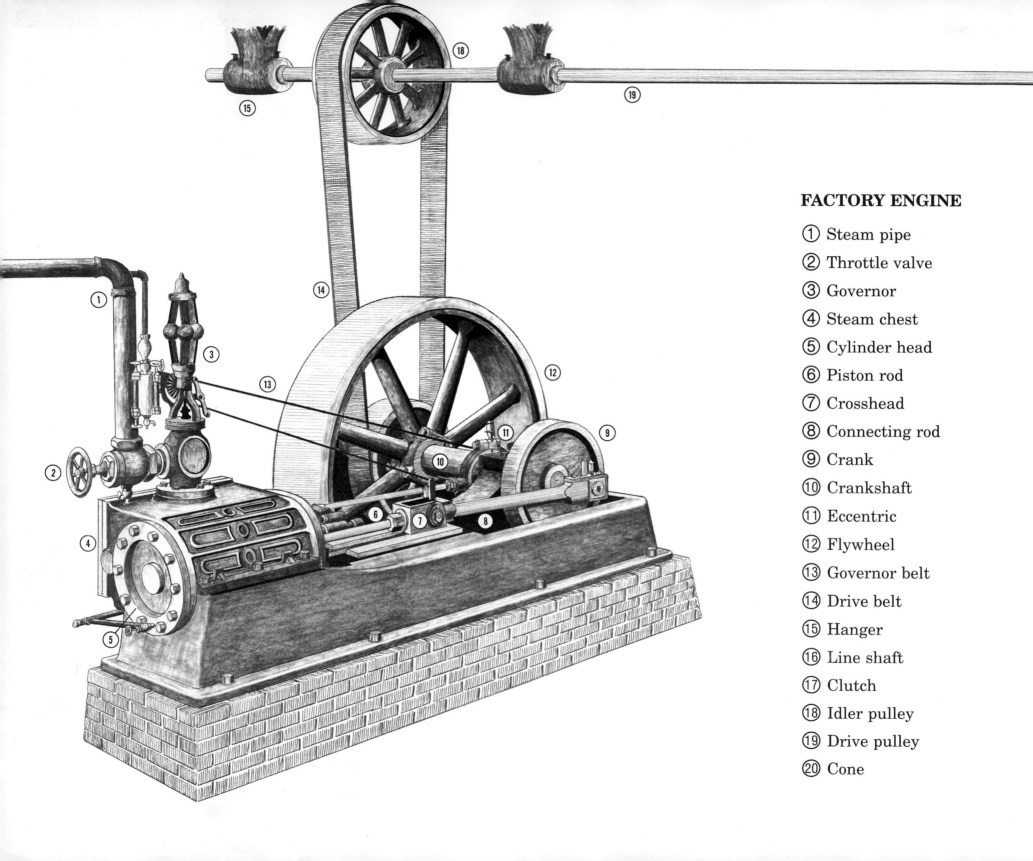

FACTORY ENGINE

1. Steam pipe
2. Throttle valve
3. Governor
4. Steam chest
5. Cylinder head
6. Piston rod
7. Crosshead
8. Connecting rod
9. Crank
10. Crankshaft
11. Eccentric
12. Flywheel
13. Governor belt
14. Drive belt
15. Hanger
16. Line shaft
17. Clutch
18. Idler pulley
19. Drive pulley
20. Cone

By the 1870s, steam engines have replaced waterwheels as the power source in factories. Steam engines grind flour and corn, spin cotton and wool yarns and weave them into cloth, pump water, run printing presses, thresh wheat, and saw lumber.

Every plant has a powerhouse containing steam engines and boilers, marked by towering brick smokestacks. Large factories, like a locomotive works, have several engines. A leather belt runs from a pulley on the steam engine up to a pulley on an overhead shaft attached to the ceiling. This long shaft carries power all over the factory. The machine shop has its own steam engine driving over a thousand feet of line shafting and five hundred pulleys.

Since the shaft is running all the time, the operator must start and stop his machine tool with a clutch. The machinist moves a wooden handle reaching up to a clutch, sliding the belt from the idler to the drive pulley. When he wants to stop his machine, he moves the belt back onto the idler. When the operator wants to change the speed of his machine tool, he stops it and then shifts the belt from one size pulley to another.

The shops hum with the spinning shafts and the *slapslapslapslap* of the long belts. Most of the locomotive is made with three machine tools: drill presses, lathes, and planers.

The drill press (*center*) drills the many hundreds of holes for bolts and rivets. This is the first machine tool assigned to young apprentices, after they have learned to read drawings and mastered hand tools such as scrapers and files.

The lathe rotates a piece of metal against a tool that makes it round. This is called turning. It also cuts screw threads and bores holes. The machinist on the left is turning an axle for the locomotive's big driving wheels from a rough piece of metal. As the metal rotates, the tool moves

from one end to the other and makes it a perfectly round cylinder. The machinist chooses different tools to make rough and fine cuts, and can polish the metal so smoothly that it becomes like a mirror.

The planer is used for making flat surfaces, such as the main and side rods, and for cutting slots. The rod is clamped down to the table. The machinist adjusts the tool for the first cut and then turns on the planer. The table glides back and forth under the tool, planing off long strips of metal. After each cut, the tool moves over and makes another cut right next to the previous one, producing a smooth surface. There are large planers that can machine engine frames more than twenty feet long.

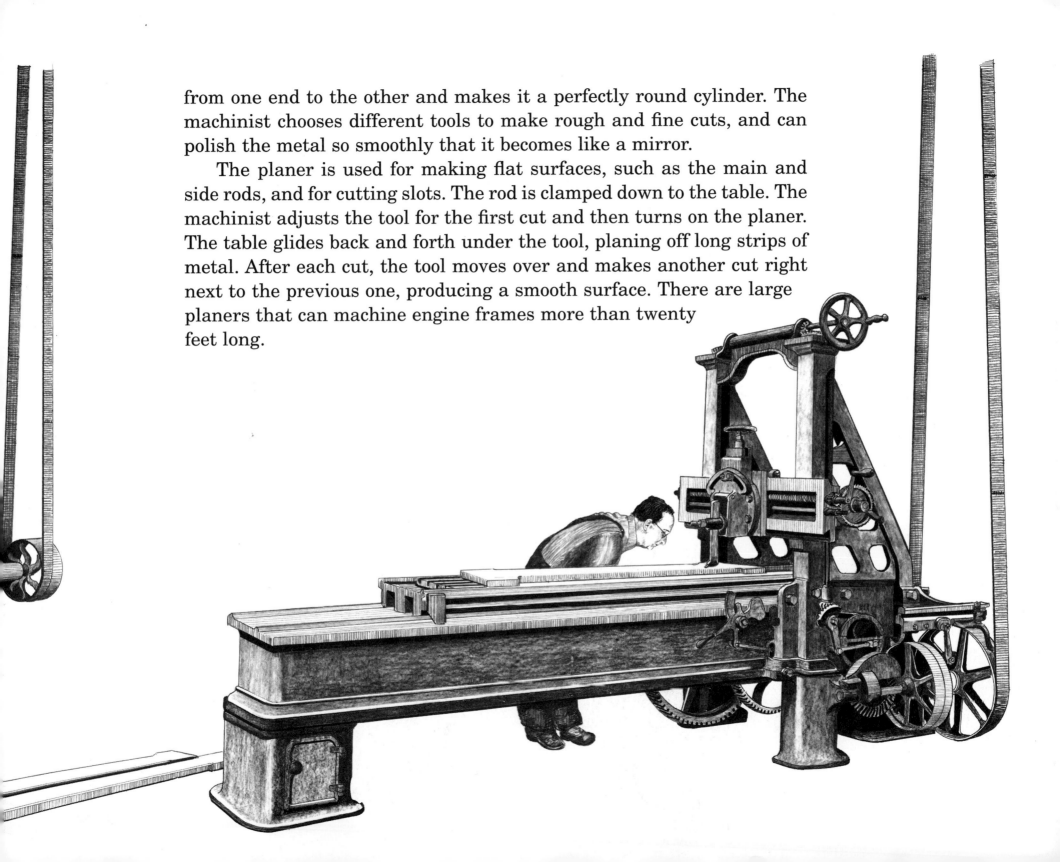

This very large lathe, called a wheel lathe, is used for turning the large wheels that drive the locomotive. The largest drivers, for high-speed passenger locomotives, are up to eighty-six inches in diameter.

The cast-iron drivers, mounted on their axle, are centered, and the cutting tool is set against the rim of a wheel. As the wheel turns, the tool shapes it. This lathe is also used for turning the tires, steel rings that will be fitted onto the wheel centers. Steel wears better than cast iron, so it is used for the tire that rolls directly on the rail.

The tires must fit tightly on the wheel centers. The machinist makes the outside diameter of the wheel center slightly bigger than the inside diameter of the tire. When the tires are heated in a round furnace, they expand and can be fitted onto the wheel center. Wheel and tire are then plunged into a vat of cold water, cooling and shrinking the tire tightly onto the wheel center.

Between the spokes on one side of the drivers are the counterbalance weights. The weights are opposite and equal in weight to the crank pin and heavy main and connecting rods, making the wheel balanced.

Steam locomotives are classified by their wheel arrangements— starting with the number of wheels in the leading truck (the small wheels that guide the locomotive around curves), followed by the number of drivers, and then the number of wheels in the trailing truck. Each type also has a name. Here are a few examples of early locomotives:

0-4-0 Four-wheel switcher
2-6-0 Mogul
2-6-2 Prairie
2-8-0 Consolidation
4-4-0 Eight-wheeler or American
4-4-2 Atlantic
4-6-0 Ten-wheeler

The line shaft continues into the forge shop, where it runs the drop hammer. A chunk of metal called an ingot is heated until it becomes bright red and soft. The blacksmith places the hot ingot on the anvil and sets the hammer in motion, lifting and then dropping it with a resounding clunk. As the metal begins to cool, the smith reheats and hammers it until it is the shape he wants. This repeated heating and hammering also makes the iron stronger.

From the adjoining smithy comes the ringing of scores of hammers on iron. Blacksmiths move back and forth between their fires and anvils, hammering out small iron parts. Bending iron bars and rods around the pointed horn of the anvil, the smith makes complete circles for tool handles, decorative work, and chain links. On the anvil's face he hammers out all kinds of small fittings.

A smith makes a sharp bend in an iron bar by putting one end into the hardie hole—a square hole in the top of the anvil—and pushing down on the other. The other smith and his helper use a swage, a grooved tool that forms round rods. They'll use a hexagonal swage to form six-sided stock, which can be cut into short lengths and made into nuts and bolts.

Smiths also weld on the anvil. The heated ends of the two pieces to be joined are held one on top of the other and hammered until they are welded together.

While forgings in the past were made under drop hammers and by muscular, hammer-wielding smiths, the really big forgings needed for locomotives are now being done with steam hammers.

The engine frame is made of iron bars hammered into shape from big ingots. To join two pieces, the end of the shorter piece is heated in the fire. The longer piece is heaped with coals in the area where the weld is to be made. When both pieces are soft, they are welded together under the heavy blows of the steam hammer.

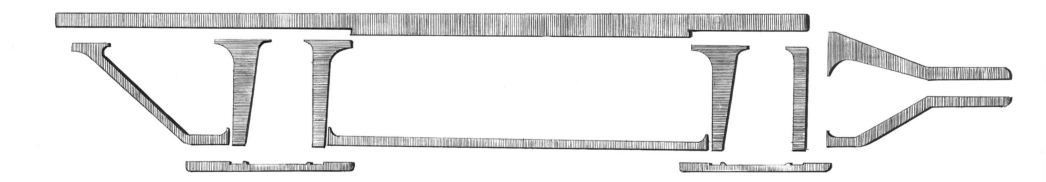

The locomotive's axles, piston rods, side and main rods, valve gear, and other parts are also forged on the steam hammer. Although these hammers wallop huge iron ingots with a force of 15,000 pounds, proud steam hammermen sometimes show off their skill by placing a hickory nut on the anvil and then striking it just hard enough to crack the shell, leaving the nutmeat whole.

In the boiler shop, sheets of iron as thick as a child's finger are cut to size by giant scissor-like shears. Hundreds of holes are punched into the sheets, which are then placed on huge rollers and shaped into the boiler sections and firebox.

The holes are for the rivets that hold the sections of this boiler together. A young apprentice takes the glowing-hot rivets from the heater with tongs and throws them to the holder-on crouched inside the boiler. The holder-on places the shank of the rivet into a hole and quickly backs it up with his hammer. A burly boilermaker hammers mightily on the other end of the rivet with a sledge indented to give each rivet a uniform mushroom or cone shape.

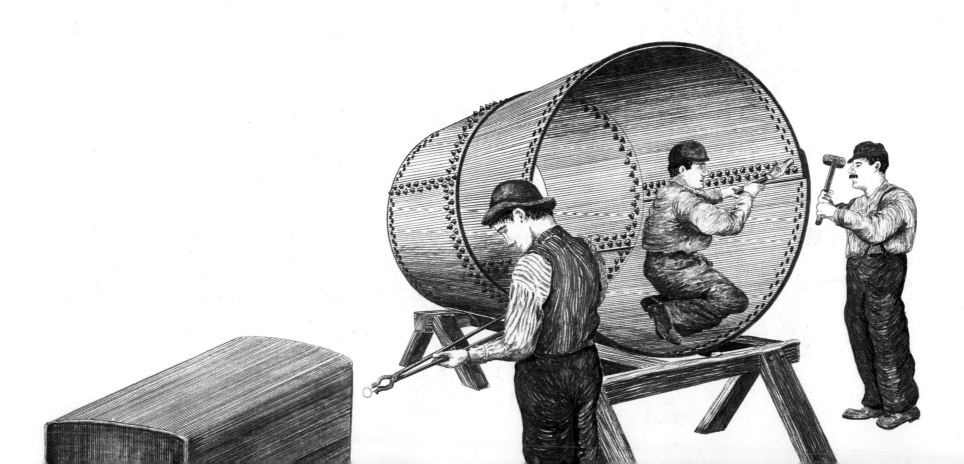

From the iron foundry come cast-iron driving wheels and 3,000-pound cylinders, as well as the delicate filigree brackets that will support the headlight. From the brass foundry come the locomotive's graceful bell, whistle, domes, and fittings for the boiler and cab.

Each piece begins in the pattern shop as a wooden model of the finished casting. This pattern is then given to a molder, who buries it in tightly packed damp sand in two open boxes called the drag and cope.

① The molder places one-half of a bell pattern into the drag, ② fills it with sand, and rams the sand tightly against the pattern and the drag.

③ Next, the molder turns over the drag, so that the pattern shows on top.

④ He puts the second box, or cope, on top of the drag and sets the other half of the bell pattern in place.

Then he fills up the cope with sand, ramming it just as he did the drag. He sticks two wooden pins into the sand, which, when they are pulled out, leave holes called the sprue and the vent.

⑤ When the molder lifts the cope off the drag, he sees the two halves of the bell pattern. He taps the pattern all around, to loosen it from the sand, and carefully lifts each piece out. Then he cuts a little channel connecting the two holes with the bell-shaped hollow . . . and closes up the mold.

⑥ All this time, brass has been melting in a furnace. The molten brass is let out into a ladle and poured down into the sprue until metal appears in the vent. That's how they know the mold is full.

After the casting has cooled, it is broken out of the sand and sent to the machine shop, where it is put on a lathe and turned until it is smooth and shiny.

The tender is taking shape in another shop. The tender stores the locomotive's fuel and water. This locomotive will burn cordwood (in the eastern United States, engines usually burn coal, which is readily available). Water is stored in the tender tank, connected by a hose to the locomotive. Both the fireman and the engineer watch the water glasses in the cab, which show them the water level in the boiler. If the water level gets too low, the fireman turns on the pump and the injector valve, forcing water into the boiler under pressure.

The tender also has a toolbox, with everything needed to make repairs and adjustments to the locomotive out on the line.

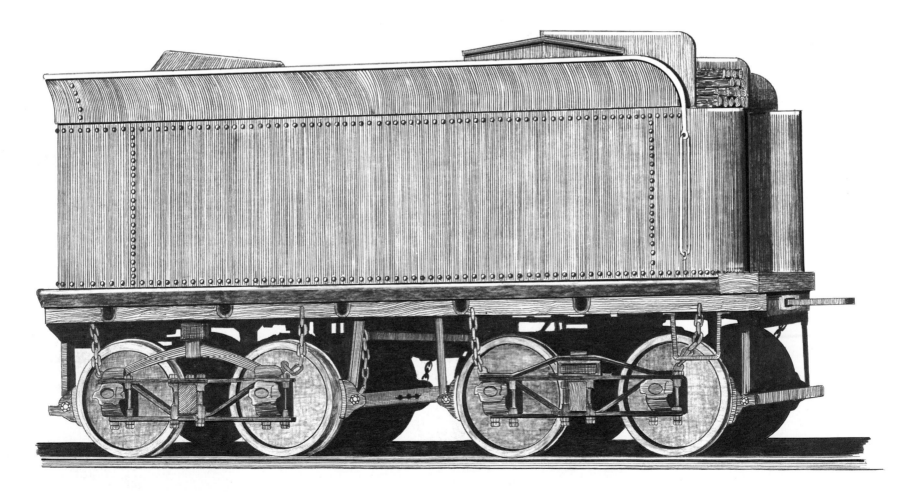

The eight-wheeler is built partly of wood. Heavy timbers make up the tender frame, pilot beam, and cowcatcher. Wood is also used for boiler insulation, footboards running along the sides of the boiler, and the beautiful cab, fashioned of varnished and polished oak, pine, and walnut. The cab houses the engineer and fireman on their long journeys, day and night, through all kinds of weather. Here they take their meals and drop off to sleep. No wonder such pride and care go into these little homes.

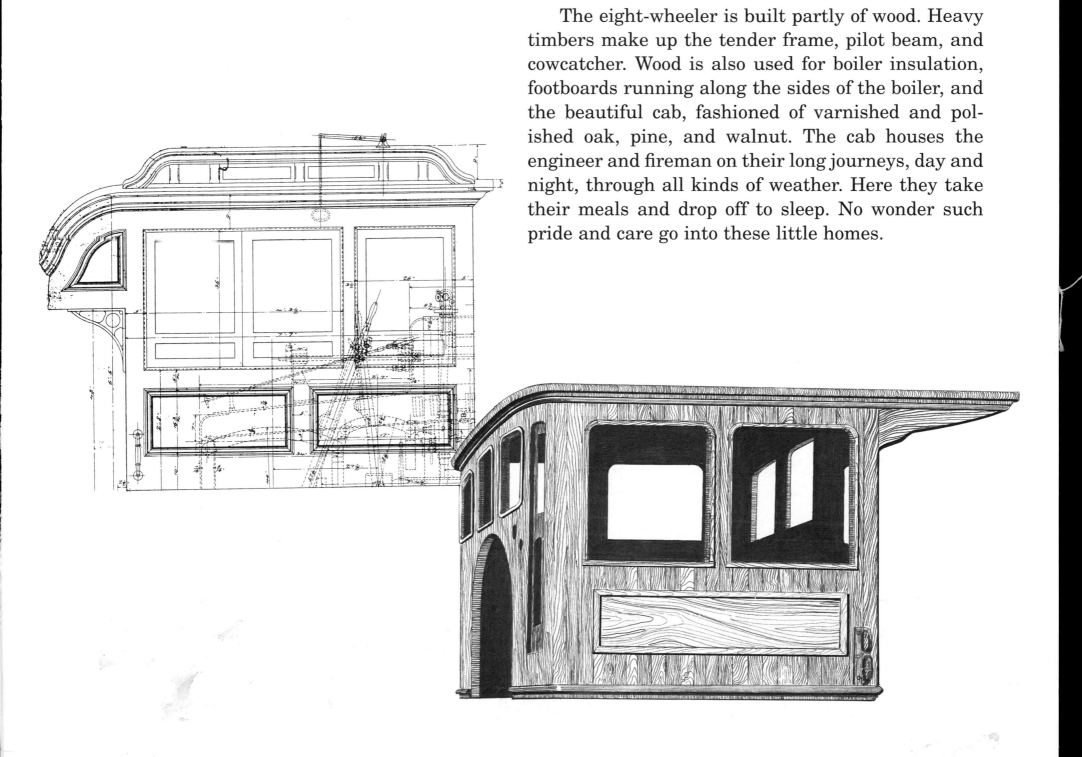

The thousands of parts that will become a new eight-wheeler pile up in the erecting shop, looking like a locomotive model kit dumped out of its box. The work begins with setting up and loosely bolting together the side frames on piles of timbers. Screw jacks are placed under the frames and adjusted until the frames are perfectly level and aligned with each other. Once this is done, the bolts are tightened to make a rigid foundation for the locomotive. The overhead crane brings the cylinders. As one gang bolts them to the frame, another team assembles the valve gear.

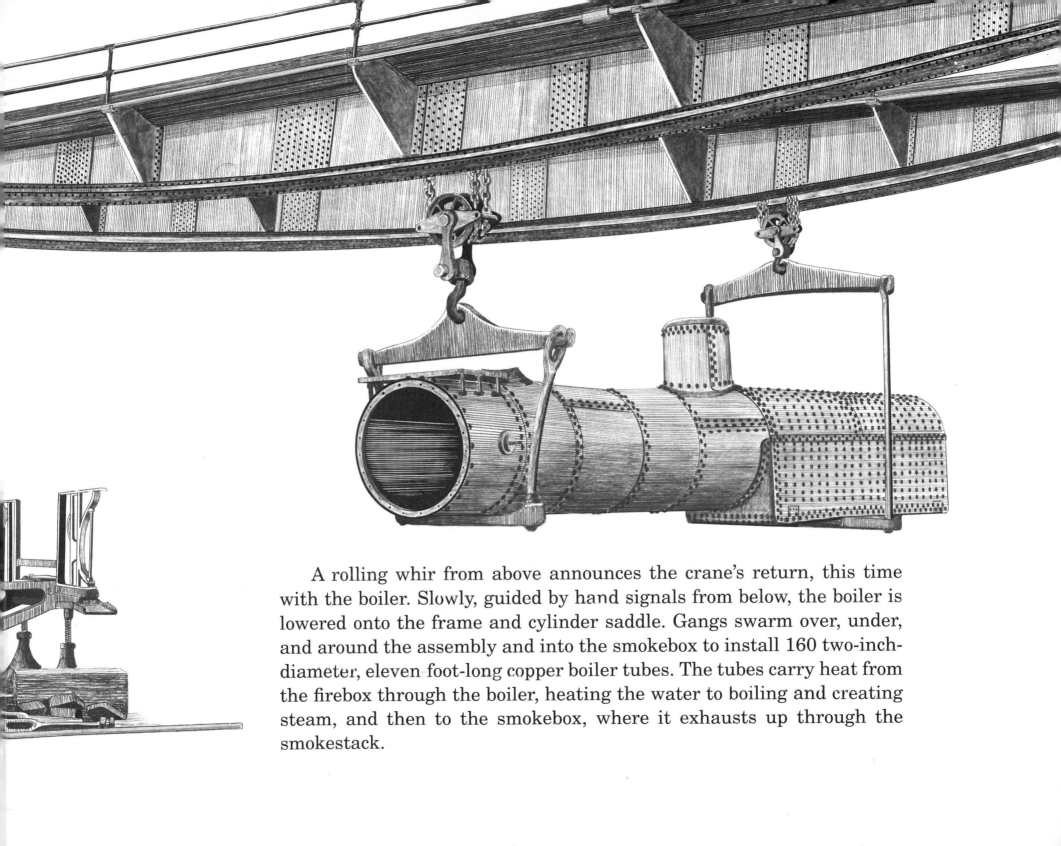

A rolling whir from above announces the crane's return, this time with the boiler. Slowly, guided by hand signals from below, the boiler is lowered onto the frame and cylinder saddle. Gangs swarm over, under, and around the assembly and into the smokebox to install 160 two-inch-diameter, eleven foot-long copper boiler tubes. The tubes carry heat from the firebox through the boiler, heating the water to boiling and creating steam, and then to the smokebox, where it exhausts up through the smokestack.

The huge erecting shop bustles with hundreds of men working on several locomotives in all stages of construction. It takes about a week to assemble one locomotive.

Despite the skill that has gone into making each part, it takes careful handwork to fit them together perfectly. Machinists make all the final adjustments with files, scrapers, and emery cloth, down to the last thousandths of an inch, painstakingly hand fitting each part into place.

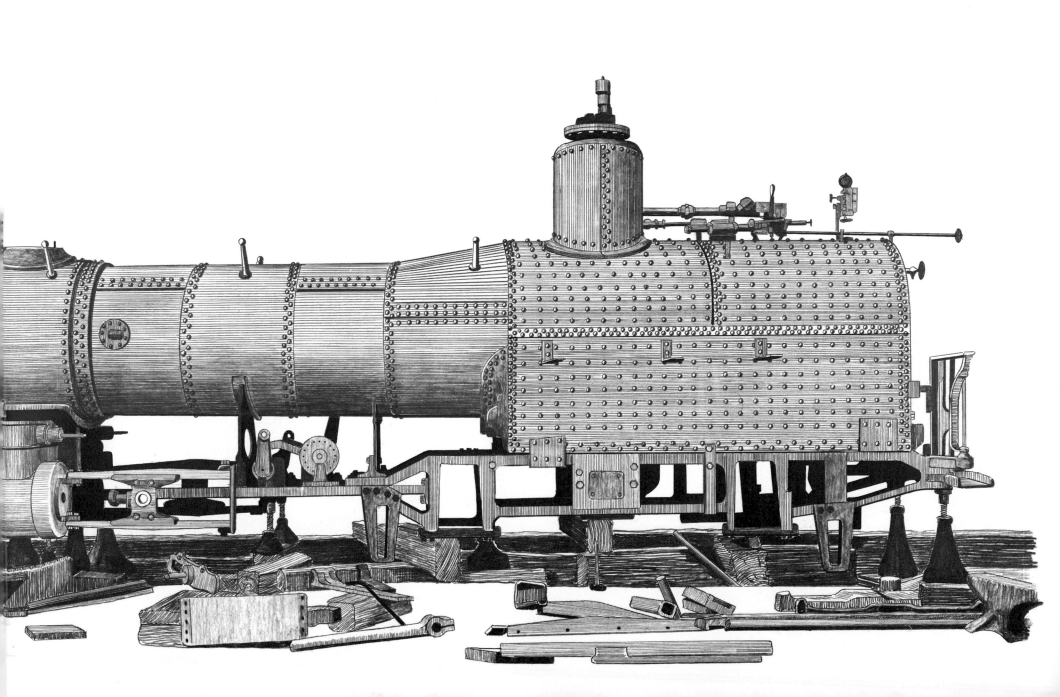

Now the entire assembly—boiler, cylinders, frame, and all—is lifted while the lead truck and drivers are rolled underneath.

The crane brings the cab, handsomely varnished. The main and side rods are attached to the drive wheels. The boiler is filled with hot water, and boilermakers check the seams to make sure there are no leaks. If a leak is found, the seam is tightened with a hammer and chisel-like tool, which forces iron into the opening and tightens the seam.

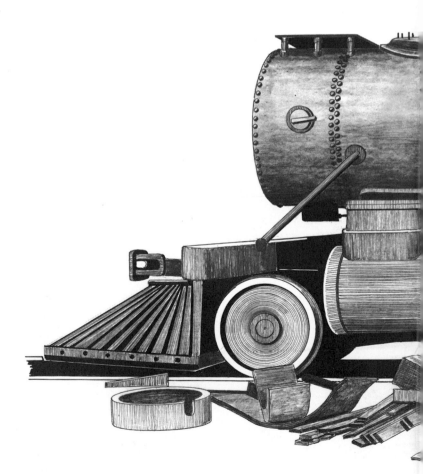

The locomotive is complete. It's been about eight weeks since the first drawings went out to the shops. The valve gear is adjusted just right, so the engine will run smoothly and get the most power out of each cylinderful of steam. The boiler is tested again, this time with live steam from the shop boiler, at 125 pounds per square inch. The tender arrives, is coupled to the engine, and the water lines are connected between them. Painters arrive with brushes and paints to apply lettering and numbers.

Number 220, shiny black, with the sun glinting off its brass bell and whistle, steams out of the shop on its six-foot drivers and onto a siding to await shipment. Soon the locomotive will be coupled into a long freight train and pulled across the country to a waiting engineer and fireman, who will keep it polished, oiled, and smooth-running as this first day out of the shops.

To tell this story, I needed the help of friends who sent me drawings and photographs, demonstrated the workings of machine tools, and patiently answered my unending questions about locomotive-building. So I'd like to thank Kyle Wyatt and Christopher Dewitt of the Nevada State Railroad Museum; Ellen Halteman, librarian, California State Railroad Museum; John K. Brown; Peter Vogt; Bruce Hepler; Sam Thompson; Andy Fahrenwald; and Peter Barton, Altoona Railroaders Memorial Museum. And a special thanks to Walter Gray III, who many years ago gave me an article on early locomotive builders and encouraged me to do this book.

The text of this book is set in New Century Schoolbook.
The illustrations are pen and ink, and pencil.

Library of Congress Cataloging-in-Publication Data

Weitzman, David L.
Locomotive : building an eight-wheeler / David Weitzman.
p.   cm.
ISBN 0-395-69687-9
1. Locomotives — United States — History.   I. Title.
TJ603.2.W45   1999
625.26'1'0973 — dc21   99-10815   CIP

Manufactured in the United States of America
HOR 10 9 8 7 6 5 4 3 2 1

Ash pan ㉚
Back driving wheels ㉜
Bell ⑥⑥
Bell cord ⑥⑦
Boiler ㊾
Cab ㊵

Cab foot steps ㊱
Cab front door ㊶
Cab handholds ㊴
Cab support ㊾
Cladding plate band ㉗
Cleanout ⑦⓪

Connecting rod ㉑
Counterbalance weights ㉖
Coupling rod ㉔
Cowcatcher ⑥
Crosshead ⑯
Crosshead guide bar ⑰

Cylinder ⑩
Cylinder cocks ⑮
Dome ㊻
Draw bar ㊳
Driving springs ㉗
Driving wheel guard ㉞

Equalizing lever ㉙
Expansion link ㉒
Firebox ㉛
Flag holder ④
Footboard ㉝
Furnace door ㊾